CUTE ANIMAL COLORING BOOK

This Book Belongs To:

Looking for a fun, adorable, creative, kids coloring book filled with super cute animals? The Cute Animal Coloring Book is perfect for toddlers and children aged 3-8 years.

It is filled with brave lions, tigers, and cheetahs, plus purrfect pets, fantastic farm animals and cute sleeping sloths. The coloring book contains 50 unique drawings ranging from easy to expert, enabling your child to choose the level that appeals to them.

From Janelle x

www.jmcgbooks.com

ISBN: 978-0-6483094-5-1

Copyright © 2021

All rights reserved. No part of this publication may be reproduced, distributed or transmitted in any form or by any means including photocopying, recording, or other electronical or mechanical methods, without the prior written permission of the publisher, except in the case of brief quotations embodied in critical reviews and certain other non commerical uses permitted by copyright law.

LEVEL 1
EASY

LEVEL 2
MEDIUM

LEVEL 3
EXPERT

Thank you for purchasing this coloring book!

I hope you enjoyed this coloring book as much as I enjoyed creating it. If you liked this book, I'd be really appreciative if you could spare a couple of minutes to write an online review. Reviews and feedback mean so much and I'd love to hear your thoughts.

Thank you, Janelle x

Other books by Janelle McGuinness:

Unicorn, Rainbows, Mermaids and More

Beneath the Tranquil Sea

Mission 1 – Lost Lunchboxes

Come Out Mr Poo!

My First Day at DayCare

Potty Time for Boys

Potty Time for Girls

www.jmcgbooks.com

Made in the USA
Las Vegas, NV
17 August 2021